CW00641191

Early 1900's fashions in Dundee.

Spratters in Dundee Harbour
1950's

Phillips

DUNDEE

ₒₒₒ *a city made of memories*

Douglas Phillips and Ron Thompson

Illustrations © Douglas Phillips
Text © Ron Thompson
Printed and published by David Winter & Son Ltd
Block 16
Dunsinane Avenue
Dunsinane Industrial Estate
Dundee
September 1993

ISBN 0 902804 23 5

Doug

Photography by Ron Gazzard, Dundee

Ron

Dundee is a city well-regarded for its artists and writers and among their ranks the work of Doug Phillips and Ron Thompson has been much in evidence over the past forty-odd years. Both are local men who sampled clerical life in the jute industry before initially achieving their vocational goals in the newspaper and magazine empire of D. C. Thomson & Co. Ltd.

Since 1966 Doug has been a freelance artist. His oils and watercolours are to be seen regularly at leading exhibitions throughout the country and several of his paintings have become popular limited edition prints. His drawings of Dundee past and present are particularly well-known and, together with illustrations in over a hundred children's books, have brought him recognition in many parts of the world.

Ron has had an equally varied career. After working on several national newspapers, including the "Daily Herald" and "Sunday Express", he returned to Dundee where he later joined Grampian Television as their locally-based reporter. When he retired from that post, after 26 years in front of camera, he was awarded the M.B.E. for services to television journalism. He is the author of several books and is now a freelance writer and broadcaster.

INTRODUCTION

When Doug Phillips and I were asked in 1991 to collaborate in a book of drawings and text about old Dundee we little realised that our joint venture would gradually develop into a series. But that is what has happened. Following our second volume in 1992 we were once again encouraged by public response to forge ahead and complete the trilogy. This we have done with the book now before you. This third offering, like the others, takes you on a dauner back through time to be remembered of people, places, and customs, whose earlier existence is part of all our yesterdays. Who can ever forget, for example, the D.E.C.S. (the "Sosh"), the Labour Exchange (the "Broo"), the bustle of South Union Street, Victoria Road, and Hawkhill, and the knock on the door from the Onion ("Ingin") Johnnies and the Arbroath fishwives? Dundonians hold their own opinions about their own city but two things can be clearly stated without fear of contradiction: Dundee, which has changed out of all recognition over the past 35 years, has a tremendously rich heritage of folk history – and its people like nothing more than to talk about the old times. If there was a Scottish Cup for nostalgia Dundee folk who remember these byegone days would at least be in the final. Enjoy that experience now as we wish you yet another happy and evocative journey back into the past.

Ron Thompson,
September, 1993

CONTENTS

The old Overgate plagues the memories of ageing Dundonians more than any other part of the former city. Being the most central of all the precincts it attracted the greatest numbers, thus creating a character and atmosphere unmatched elsewhere in Dundee at that time.

In the beginning the Overgate was populated with the mansion houses of rich merchants. Latterly it was a warren of narrow cobbled streets, closes, alleys, pends, and back courts, which were filled with crumbling tenement houses above and behind ragged rows of fondly-remembered shops. The Overgate, as seen on the right prior to its demolition in 1962, stretched westwards from Boots on one corner and the Sixty Minute Cleaners on the other.

The rounded tower of General Monk's headquarters dominated the entrance until this symbol of the English invasion in 1651 finally fell to a bulldozer over three hundred years later. Latterly, tucked in at the left before coming to Keith Scott's, was a high-speed barber's shop with seven chairs, operated on a conveyor belt system by Tommy Gibson. It was claimed you could have a haircut here in the time it took the barman in The Pump across the street to pour a couple of pints of beer., Put another way, your short-back-and-sides would be completed before your coat had stopped swinging on the rack.

This was all in stark contrast to the timeless atmosphere in an earlier salon further up the Overgate run by the famous Pat Fletcher, a local magistrate with a great appetite for debate. A haircut there could last most of the afternoon as topical events were given a thorough airing. But Gibson's had memorable moments as well. On one occasion a man who came in with a young lad had the full treatment: haircut, shave, face massage, whiskers singed, and a shampoo. The customer then asked for the boy's hair to be trimmed while he popped over the road for a pint. He would square up for everything when he came back.

When finished with the boy the barber told him to take a seat until his father returned. "Faither?", said the lad. "He's no' mey faither. E've never seen him afore. He just stopped me ootside and said that if eh came in here wi' him eh would get to read the coamics." The bill came to 17s 6d. Needless to say the well-groomed gent had done a runner and was never seen again.

A "quickie" at Gibson's.

Foot of Overgate.

Mid Overgate.

There was Fagan the pawnbroker, Reilly's Amusement Arcade, the Tom Thumb Fruit Bazaar, Palmer's rock shop, Maurice Rosen the house furnisher, Birrell's and Patterson's fighting it out over shoes, tripe shops, second-hand shops, shops that offered a "threepenny roll-up" – a cigarette, match, and dash of wine. And who could forget the wee shoppies between Tally Street and Lindsay Street, all below ground level and offering marvellous bargains in fruit, candy, and monster mutton pies. Yes, the retail reach of the Overgate was endless. There was even a chemist's shop which was famous for its health drinks. It was called Greenhill's, seen here on the left in the middle part of the precinct, and it was there you drank coloured concoctions of various flavours, all fizzed up with spoonfuls of white powder. The speciality of the house was Sarsparilla, better known as a "Sass", which was the colour and taste of liquorice:

> "Sugarelly water, black as the lum,
>   Gather up your preens and ye'll a' get some."

Greenhill's was established in the Overgate at the turn of the century by a Glasgow man, James Greenhill, who had switched careers to become a chemist and later create his unique range of refreshments. Sarsparilla was certainly the big favourite with Boston Cream not far behind. During a heatwave in 1912 there was a record sale of 9000 "Sasses" over several weeks. When Mr Greenhill died in 1948 at the age of 84 he was Dundee's oldest chemist. At No. 219 Overgate there was the Salvation Army Slum Headquarters where much sustenance, spiritual and material, was dispensed to those in need. Poverty was to be seen in this quarter of the city wherever you looked but those who lived in the Overgate, in backlands like these on the right, had their own fierce sense of pride, as exemplified in the following exchange between a grandmother and her grandson: "This is an affie oarrie place ye bide in Grannie Nellie", said the eight-year-old on one of his visits to the Overgate. "It's no' an oarrie place at a' laddie", retorted the old woman. "It's the oarrie fowk who come aboot it that gies it the name."

Backlands.

Barrack Street.

Barrack Street (left) ran from Ward Road down to the Overgate at which junction Tally Street (right) took over to continue the passage south to the Nethergate. Barrack Street accommodated a rich variety of commercial enterprises . . . a textile mill, the Inland Revenue, Investment Trusts, Sheriff Officers, pubs, a jeweller, plumber, draper, and hairdresser. At the top end it bordered – as it still does – the ancient burial ground of the Howff. Indeed, when the Howff opened as a cemetery Barrack Street, originally named Friar's Vennel, then became known as Burial Wynd and only changed to its present name in 1807 when Barrack Street seemed a more fitting description for a thoroughfare so close to Dudhope Castle which by then was occupied by the military. One of the street's top attractions was Frank Russell's book shop which stocked tomes on every conceivable subject, particularly in the field of education. Students would throng this treasure house for their reading matter, at times queuing up on the pavement to gain access. Many returned to the city in later life for a nostalgic browse round the famous bookshop. Other customers included Ramsay MacDonald, Britain's first Labour prime minister, and Fritz Kreisler, the acclaimed Austrian violinist.

Frank Russell had been a scholarly young man whose interest in books led him to an apprenticeship in book-binding with the old Dundee firm of William Kidd where he rose to the position of manager. Later he also managed Victoria Printing Works before setting up his shop at the beginning of the First World War. In 1927 he opened a second outlet in the City Arcade, both premises carrying a total stock of 30,000 books. Mr Russell, who was also an ardent church and mission worker, preached in over sixty churches. He died in 1959 aged 84. Tally Street boasted one of Dundee's oldest hotels, the New Imperial, previously known as the City Hotel. It shared this street with Wilkie the butcher; Miss Roy, fruiterer; John Young, house furnishers; and, of course, Miss Peebles, the draper's shop at the corner with the Nethergate, one of the city's best-known fashion centres from the twenties to the sixties. On the other side of Tally Street, fronting the Nethergate, are the city churches contained within a period building. One of the distinguishing features of this precinct is the ancient tree at the rear of St. Mary's, a survivor in a much-changed landscape.

Tally Street.

The Hawkhill (right), to be forever known as the "Hackie", was, like the Overgate, Wellgate, and Hilltown, a self-contained central enclave of distinctive character: a village within a city. It stretched right back from the West Port to the Sinderins at Perth Road, a distance of less than a mile but a community tightly jammed with tenements, factories, and shops of every description. The Hawkhill catered for all the necessities of life. You could have spent an entire lifetime there without ever once having to journey beyond its boundaries. Indeed, youngsters were at one time warned never to go beyond the West Port unless accompanied by an adult. These were the days when shops vied for custom by offering services beyond their normal obligations. For example, one Hawkhill chemist had a notice in the window which said: "Teeth carefully extracted." The letters were formed by teeth already removed from patients at a shilling a session – without an anaesthetic. Another chemist had a certain reputation as a skin specialist. He was

Bernard Street.

Bailie McKinnon, one of several Hawkhill shopkeepers who served on the town council in the early part of the century, the others including Bailie McCabe, the baker; Bailie Wood, draper; and Bailie Quirk, a barber. Hawkhill also had its full quota of licensed premises – 18 grocers and 14 pubs – and a number of cinemas, notably the State in Bellfield Street, now the Whitehall Theatre, and the Princess, originally the Hippodrome, which closed in 1959. The other great place of entertainment in the Hackie was the West End Palais in Well Road, more fondly known as "Robbies" after is founder John Robertson. Thousands of young Dundonians learned ballroom dancing there to the strict tempo records of dance band leaders like Victor Sylvester. Robbies basically consisted of two rooms, one for dancing and the other for sitting and chatting. Hawkhill has also made a remarkable impact in a rather more unlikely field: the world of athletics. Hawkhill Harriers were founded in 1889 by several local working lads with a love of running. The club went on to introduce the famous Perth to Dundee road race and to form a ladies section in 1928 which, fifty years later, was to develop the talents of Liz McColgan, one of the world's leading middle and long-distance runners. In fact Hawkhill Harriers have been represented by a number of athletes at Commonwealth and Olympic Games level.

The Hawkhill was intersected by many interesting lanes, wynds, streets, and roads, none more so than Bernard Street (left) whose residents had the reputation of staging the city's most impressive celebrations at times of national rejoicing. At the 1937 Coronation of King George VI and Queen Elizabeth, Bernard Street was so awash with flags, emblems, portraits, bunting, and fairy lights, that people came from miles around just to admire the patriotic display which, by popular demand, wasn't dismantled until three weeks after the crowning ceremony. Again at the victory celebrations to mark the end of war in 1945, and at the present Queen's Coronation in 1953, Bernard Street was declared the outstanding city street in overall decoration. Hawkhill can be traced back to about 1490 when it was the main access to Dundee from the west before the advent of Perth Road. This area may then have been devoted to the sport of hawking, hence the name Hawkhill. Today it is only a shell of its former self, most of it having been demolished to form part of the campus of Dundee University, established in 1967. What is left is largely by-passed by a modern road system.

Hawkhill.

15

Premierland.

Dundee was once a big boxing centre, producing an impressive pool of professional and amateur champions and staging many important title fights at indoor and outdoor venues throughout the city. By the early 1930's it had a boxing stadium of its own, Premierland, just off William Lane which ran between King Street and Victoria Road. It began as an open-air arena drawing crowds of up to 1700 before being enclosed under a circus top. Later, after the canvas roof collapsed under a heavy fall of snow, the marquee was replaced by a former aircraft hanger. For nearly thirty years Premierland hosted boxing tournaments, wrestling matches, and a variety of other events before finally ending its days as an indoor golf driving range. On one memorable occasion in October, 1952, it staged a title event with a difference – an attempt to set up a new individual world record for non-stop piano playing by the remarkable Sandy Strickland from Bolton in Lancashire. "Syncopating Sandy", as he was known, already held the record of 176 hours. For nearly eight days thousands packed the stadium as the marathon musician tinkled the ivories for hours on end, playing almost every number that had ever been composed. When he finally established a new record of 180 hours a cheering crowd of 10,000, crammed into surrounding streets, carried him shoulder-high to a waiting taxi.

Premierland's development was the brainchild of George P. Grant, one of Dundee's best-known and popular figures of his time. He started working life by selling newspapers in the street, rapidly becoming Dundee's top vendor and thereby qualifying to occupy the most lucrative pitches – a determination to succeed which was to manifest itself throughout his colourful career. George went on to become a bookmaker and over the years built up a successful chain of betting shops throughout Dundee and Angus. But it was as a boxing promoter, and his determination to put Dundee on the fight map, that turned him into a national figure. It is said that he first became involved in the business side of the sport while at a football match in Dundee. A group of fans beside him argued throughout the game about the respective merits of two local boxers. George said he would settle the controversy by matching them in a public contest. This he seemingly did, made a profit, and never looked back. Eventually he was staging fights throughout Scotland and in 1946 promoted the world flyweight championship between the title holder, Jackie Paterson, of Glasgow, and Joe Curran, of Liverpool. The bout took place at Hampden Park and set a world record outdoor attendance at that time of 50,000. Paterson won on points over 15 rounds. Many years later this great champion fought for the last time in Scotland at Premierland, being beaten on points by local fighter Willie Myles, before emigrating to South Africa where he met a violent death in 1966 in a stabbing incident. George Grant, as head of G. P. Grant's Promotions, was well-respected in the business community. Each year he held an outing for hundreds of local youngsters which became known as "Geordie's picnic". George was interested in many sports and, as a participant, excelled in curling. In 1960 he skipped a family rink consisting of his two sons and daughter to reach the quarter-finals of the world championships in Edinburgh. He was also a director of Dundee Ice Rink. George Grant, Dundee's boxing ambassador, died in October 1966, aged. 61

George Grant.

Glebe Street in the east end of the city is fondly remembered by thousands of Dundonians, mainly because of its proximity to Glebelands Primary School. The street disappeared many years ago but the school lives on as one of Dundee's oldest centres of primary education. Twice it has risen from the ashes, first when gutted by fire in 1912 and then when completely modernised in 1974. On both occasions the outer walls of the original school, opened in February, 1878, were preserved. The "Glebie", as it is always referred to, was at one time surrounded by the heavily-populated tenement areas of Lilybank Road, Watson Street, Ferry Road, Baffin Street, Springhill, Grove Street, Eden Street, St. Matthew Street, Arbroath Road, and, of course, Glebe Street itself. Between the two world wars it was easily the largest primary school in the east end with a roll of 1300. When war broke out again in 1939 the school was evacuated to Arbroath although by 1941 Glebelands was back in business, albeit on a part-time basis. But with the building of new perimeter council housing estates after the war, along with primary schools to cater for the families decanted from the tenementlands of urban Dundee, the Glebelands roll gradually fell. And with the closure of the Caledon Shipyard in 1981 the school's long connection with the families of shipyard workers also came to an end. The Glebie has had many respected and well-loved teachers over the years. One of these was Bob Mudie who, over seventy years ago, coached pupils who had failed their "Quali" and were in these days kept on in primary until they were fourteen. After punishing one such pupil for misbehaving, the boy threatened to bring his father up to school to sort out the teacher. "Aye, just do that", snorted Bob. "I often belted him too before you were born!" In the same era there was also Miss Templeton, a small, prim lady who presented an unforgettable spectacle in her black, knee-high gaiters, clip-clopping down Lilybank Road after school each day to board the Ferry Road tram. Pocket money then was spent in three sweetie shops almost next door to each other in Lilybank Road, including the one run by Miss Crabb, known as "Auld Crabbies". Glebe Street and Glebelands School take their names from the church land on which they were built. This ground was called a glebe and was at one time given to the parish minister to supplement his stipend.

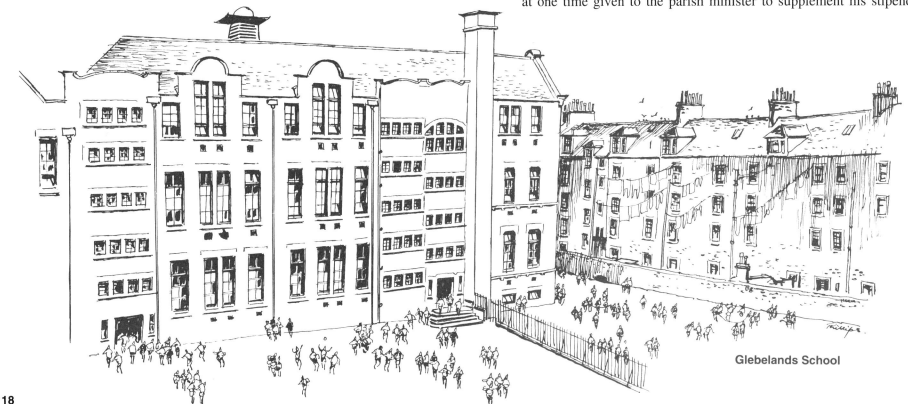

Glebelands School

For over a hundred years the "Sosh" and the "divi" were part and parcel of everyday life in Dundee. The "Sosh" was, of course, the Co-op – the D.E.C.S. (Dundee Eastern Co-operative Society Ltd) which ran an impressive chain of food stores and other shops throughout the city. Customers were members of the Society and held a nominal shareholding. The "divi" was the dividend paid to customers twice a year and was a percentage of what they had spent at the Co-op during the previous six months. ("The mair yi eat the bigger the divi".) Co-operative Societies flourished all over Britain as part of the Co-operative movement, which in turn was rooted in the greater Socialist cause. Originally they were aimed at giving working-class families a financial interest in their own retail chain and were controlled by committees, many of whose early members in the Dundee Co-op were foremen in the local jute mills and factories. Co-ops were really the forerunner of present-day supermarkets where all the weekly shopping could be carried out under the one roof. They were the grocer, butcher, and baker, all rolled into one. They offered everything from milk and coal to shoes, clothes, and furnishings – the "Sosh" had it all. The D.E.C.S. set up its first shop in Erskine Street in 1873 with a capital of £84. By 1886, with several branches then trading, there was a membership of 1750 generating annual sales of £43,000. In 1933, the Society's diamond jubilee, membership stood at 21,600 with sales of just over £1 million a year. The Society went on to develop a complex of over thirty stores – taking in the neighbouring communities of Monifieth and Invergowrie – along with a bakery, a coal depot, a wholesale unit, and a boot repair factory. The head office and central premises (below) were at the junction of Seagate and Peter Street. Here there was an extensive department store which became the focal point of one of Dundee's leading shopping centres. Members of the "Sosh" had to follow a very definite routine when they did their shopping. Customers were issued with a book in which they listed the items they required. On entering the shop the book was placed in a box on the counter. When your book reached the bottom of the pile and your name was called out it was then your turn to be served. But why was it called the "Sosh"? Possibly because it was short for "Sale of Shareholding" (the first letters of the first two words and the first two letters of the third word) which was stamped into each customer's book when they paid for their nominal holding in the company. One thing is certain. On the day the dividends were distributed – and they rose at one stage to 3s 9d in the pound, equal to 19% –other shops in the city enjoyed a bonanza. The last D.E.C.S. shop closed many years ago but the "Sosh" and the "divi" will never be forgotten.

D.E.C.S. Headquarters.

Beefcan Close.

Apart from its rather intriguing name, there was little to distinguish Beefcan Close from the hundreds of other similar pockets of tenement housing in Dundee. But where exactly was it? Some people claim it was in the area of Todburn Lane and William Lane, both of which lay between King Street and Victoria Road. Many of those who lived in this district, now redeveloped with modern housing, worked in Baxter's mill nearby. But poverty was rife and families in the close would often sell or pawn their cooking utensils to raise much-needed cash. They would then go down to the local grocer, ask for the big, empty cannisters which had previously contained processed meat, and use them as pots in which to cook their food. They were known as beef cans, hence Beefcan Close. There is, however, another account which places the close in the Overgate between Lindsay Street and Tally Street, next door to the Argentine Meat Company which sold large quantities of imported corned beef from South America in big tins. The empty cans were left for collection in bins beside the wall of the close which, naturally, became known as the Beefcan Close. Both these accounts of how the name originated carry the ring of truth – and both locations of this famous close are each supported in different versions of a famous folk song called the Beefcan Close. Perhaps there were several Beefcan Closes. In the meantime here are the words of the song, first as they locate the close in the Overgate:

Now as I went up the Overgate, I met Jemima Ross,
An' she winked at me wi' the tail o' her e'e,
In the middle o' the Beefcan Close.

Chorus
Ricky doo dum day, doo dum day,
Ricky-dicky doo dum day.

I asked her who she stayed with,
An' she said it was Mistress Bruce,
An' after that I got an in-
vitation till her hoose.

When I went up the close that nicht,
The stairs wis awfy dark,
So I took my money fae my inside pooch,
An' I tied it tae the tail o' ma sark.

When I went in the hoose that nicht,
I ower tae the chair sat doon,
But she winked at me wi' the tail o' here e'e,
An' she says, 'Come ben the room.'

Now a' that nicht I dreamt I wis in
The airms o' Jemima Ross,
But when I woke up I was on ma back
In the middle o' the Beefcan Close.

Now a' ye lads an' lassies here,
When ye gang oot for a lark,
Jist be like me when ye're on a spree,
Tie the money tae the tail o' yer sark.

An' now my song is ended here,
I hope you enjoyed it well,
An' when you go up the Overgate,
See an' enjoy yersel'.

In the second version the chorus remains the same and the words in the main body of the song differ only slightly. But the opening two verses clearly identify the close as being towards the east end of the city as follows:

As I gaed up the Overgate, feelin' affy dry,
I met a lass an' wi' had a gless,
But mind lads, I was fly.

I asked her what her name was, says she, 'Jemima Ross,
I live awa' in Todburn Lane,
At the back o' the Beefcan Close.'

No doubt the whereabouts of the original Beefcan Close will stir many an argument for years to come.

"The stairs wis awfy dark."

Evacuees.

At 11 o'clock on Sunday morning, September 3rd, 1939, a minister climbed into the pulpit of his Dundee church carrying an old and battered wireless set. Balancing it on the edge of his lofty perch he twiddled with the controls until finally the voice of the Prime Minister, Neville Chamberlain, crackled out over the kirk. The congregation, straining to pick up his words, were able to hear the fateful declaration of war with Germany. But even before this official announcement of hostilities thousands of Dundee youngsters, many accompanied by their mothers and other relatives, were streaming out of the city to seek refuge from the Luftwaffe at safe havens in rural areas. The great dispersal was under way and with it a new category of person was introduced to the topsy-turvy world of that time – the evacuee. Nearly 20,000 adults and children were evacuated from Dundee over the next few years, although it was the initial mass exodus which created the searing memories of families being broken up amid scenes of high emotion. Thousands queued at the railway stations, the children with identity labels tied to their clothing, as special trains were mobilised to take them on their journeys into Angus, Perthshire, and the Mearns.

Tearful parents waved off their children. This was no Sunday school picnic. But some of the evacuees were so unsettled in their new surroundings they returned within weeks, others following only months later as the initial panic over imminent air attack gradually subsided. It was even known for families, billeted only a few miles inland from the city, to nip into town on a Saturday to go to the cinema. Dundee was, of course, a potential bombing target with its harbour, shipyard, engineering workshops, and jute factories, all geared up to the war effort. In the event the city escaped lightly, taking only 38 bombs and suffering few casualties. Apart from "evacuee" there were many other descriptive words added to the wartime lexicon on the domestic front: ration books, sandbags, air raid sirens, A.R.P. (Air Raid Precautions), wardens, firewatchers, Home Guard, utility clothing and furniture, blackout, British Restaurants, Pasha and Grand Turk cigarettes, gas masks, and, of course, air raid shelters. There were nearly 10,000 shelters of various types erected throughout the city. There were basement shelters in certain public buildings, communal domestic shelters in the streets and back-courts of tenements, trench shelters on open ground and in parks, and the individual family shelters. The latter came in two forms. There was the Morrison Shelter, a steel-framed cage standing in the kitchen which you simply crawled into. By far the more popular, however, was the Anderson Shelter (below), named after the Lord Privy Seal of the time, Sir John Anderson. These shelters came as self-assembly kits consisting of corrugated iron sheets which had to be bolted together and sunk into gardens and drying greens, the curved roofs camouflaged by strips of turf. Many of these shelters became a home-from-home equipped with bunks, carpets, primus stoves, paraffin heaters, and various forms of lighting. Alerts during the night could last several hours so a bit of comfort was no bad thing. After the war many of these shelters became gang headquarters for local youngsters. Others were converted into garden sheds and can still be seen today serving that purpose. One of Dundee's most unusual shelters was the old Law Tunnel, once used by the Dundee-Newtyle railway line. Despite being damp and gloomy, it offered protection to many residents at the top end of the city, although old folk found the climb up to the entrance an exhausting experience. They had much cause to curse Adolf Hitler.

Air raid!

During the last war the armed forces of many Allied nations were to be found in Dundee. There were French submarines at the harbour, a Norwegian seaplane base in the Tay, and Polish troops spread across the city. Quite a number of these men married local girls and settled in Dundee when peace returned in 1945. The Polish Army contingent occupied the former jute mansion of Castleroy in Broughty Ferry and established an engineering cadet base in Tay Street School. Apart from their military expertise the Poles possessed impeccable manners on the social front and captured the hearts of many Dundee women, a manoeuvre which didn't always go down well with the native males.

The river was particularly busy with naval traffic, including an R.A.F. air-sea-rescue base at Tayport equipped with high-speed motor launches. There was also much flying boat activity with Walruses stationed at the Stannergate and Catalinas operating from Woodhaven near Wormit. The latter were manned by Norwegian crews who were members of 1477 flight of the Royal Norwegian Air Force which was formed at the beginning of 1942. The Catalina flying boats were engaged in anti-submarine and convoy patrols and monitoring enemy shipping off the Norwegian coast. They also undertook cloak-and-dagger missions to their own occupied country, dropping off agents behind enemy lines and occasionally allowing their service personnel brief family reunions. The Norwegians integrated well into the local life of Newport and Wormit and even today contact is maintained between the flyers' families and their former hosts on the banks of the Tay. When the war ended and the Allied servicemen returned to their own countries another, and totally different, type of newcomer arrived in Dundee to take their place . . . prefabricated housing, better known as simply prefabs. These were sectional houses comprising largely of aluminium sheeting and were provided mainly to accommodate the families of returning servicemen. They were detached, cottage-type homes with a bit of garden front and back, front and back doors, and a small tin shed. They were variously described as the "poor man's bungalow", "rabbit hutches", and "dolls houses". But they were very popular, fulfilling the dream of many families of having a place of their own. Over 1500 prefabs were erected in Dundee, the first starting to go up in 1945. Their locations included Barnhill, Glamis Road, Craigie Drive, Strips of Craigie Road, Kingsway East, Blackshade, Elgin Street, Graham Street, and Linlathen. Originally their life expectancy was to be ten years. But there were still 680 being occupied in 1967, 90 in 1970, and although today all the local authority prefabs have long since been dismantled there are over twelve remaining in the city under owner occupation.

Prefab.

There were four types of prefabs and despite outward appearances they were remarkably spacious. Basically they consisted of an entrance hall, living room, two bedrooms, bathroom and separate toilet, an eating kitchen, airing cupboard, and built-in wardrobes. They were fitted with a fridge, cooker, and immersion heater. Prefabbers had to be tough to withstand the rigours of winter and the effects of condensation. The windows with their metal sills produced large amounts of moisture. Several tenants actually erected guttering on the inside of their windows to drain the water away through a down pipe leading to a milk bottle. Notwithstanding these drawbacks, prefab tenants regarded their homes with great affection and many were reluctant to move out to the new council estates which later mushroomed across the city.

Catalinas at Woodhaven.

Castleroy.

The rich man in his castle, the poor man at his gate . . . Nowhere in Britain was inequality in living standards to be witnessed in greater contrast than when Dundee was jute capital of the world. While mill workers lived in hovels the mill owners built their palaces and mansions – the swagger houses of conspicuous consumption – on the finest sites the city could offer. The Broughty Ferry area, a seaside resort far removed from the vulgar industrial scene, was much favoured for these monuments to wealth and power. It was here that the Gilroys and the Grimmonds engaged in a battle of the "Jones's", with each of these leading textile dynasties attempting to out-do the other. Joseph Grimmond, co-founder of Bowbridge Works, was first off the mark in 1861 when he moved into Kerbat House, an imposing residence at the bottom of Camphill Road. Six years later George Gilroy, of Tay Works, commissioned a huge mansion on the highest site in the district, a dwelling that would surpass all others in its breathtaking scale. It was called Castleroy (above), set in expansive grounds with sweeping views of the river and boasting of a hundred rooms and no fewer than 365 windows. Built in a style of Gothic grandeur, it featured a striking tower and magnificent conservatory – but the architecture and trappings couldn't match the fine taste of Gilroy's neighbour just down the road.

Carbet Castle.

Grimmond, determined not to be overshadowed, extended Kerbat House (above) with east and west wings in the French Renaissance style and renamed it Carbet Castle. The interior decorations and furnishings were the best that money could buy: period furniture, two beautiful organs, and a variety of fine French clocks. The elaborate painted ceilings and doors were executed by Charles Frechou, of Paris. Even the spitoons were works of art. Ironically both these palaces ended their days very much down at heel. Castleroy was taken over by Polish troops during the Second World War, then occupied by squatters before finally being used to house families on the Council waiting list. Eventually it was killed off by dry rot and demolished in 1955, the site and grounds disposed of for private housing. Carbet Castle also fell gradually into decline. Its demolition had begun before the war until, by 1953, only a fragment remained. This was finally a contractor's yard before the last traces of opulence were flattened by a bulldozer in 1984. The painted ceilings, however, have been saved for posterity.

Clocking in.

During the years of dark, satanic mills in Dundee the hardships suffered by the city's army of textile workers were well chronicled, graphically described, and have since been endlessly compared to the wealth and power of the famous jute barons. By 1873 Dundee had 72 mills and factories employing over 42,000 people, most of whom lived in conditions of squalor and poverty. By 1901, for example, 72 per cent of the city's population were housed in either single ends or room and kitchens.

Going back to an earlier time there are few more moving accounts of industrial travail than the following extract from the book, "Chapters in the Life of a Dundee Factory Boy", in which the author, possibly James Myles, describes how he was brought as a seven-year-old from the Angus countryside to live in Dundee in the early part of the 19th century: "*On the beginning of the fifth week I got work in a spinning mill at the Dens, which filled our hearts with joy, but so near starvation were we then that my mother had only 4½d in the world. It was on a Tuesday morning in the month of 'Lady June' that I first entered a spinning mill. The whole circumstances were strange to me. The dust, the din, the work, the hissing and roaring of one person to another, the obscene language uttered, even by the youngest, and the imperious commands harshly given by those 'dressed in a little brief authority' struck my young country heart with awe and astonishment. At that time the Twelve Hours' Factory Act had not come into operation and spinning mills were in their glory as huge instruments of demoralisation and slavery. Mercenary manufacturers, to enable them to beat more upright employers in the markets, kept their machinery and hands active fifteen and in many cases seventeen hours a day, and when tender children fell asleep under the prolonged infliction of 'work! work! work!' overseers roused them with the rod or thongs of thick leather burned at the points. The lash of the slave driver was never more unsparingly used in Carolina on the unfortunate slaves than the canes and 'whangs' of mill foremen were then used on helpless factory boys. When I went to a spinning mill I was about seven years of age. I had to get out of bed every morning at five o'clock, commence work at half-past five, drop at nine for breakfast, begin again at half-past nine, work until two, which was the dinner hour, start again at half-past two and continue until half-past seven at night.*

Such were the nominal hours; but in reality there were no regular hours: masters and managers did with us as they liked. The clocks at the factories were often put forward in the morning and back at night, and instead of being instruments for the measurement of time they were used as cloaks for cheatery and oppression. Though this was known amongst the hands all were afraid to speak and a workman then was afraid to carry a watch as it was no uncommon event to dismiss anyone who presumed to know too much about the science of horology. It was during this winter that I got the first unmerciful beating from a mill overseer. I was attending a spinning frame. It got too full in the shifting and I was unable to keep up the ends. The foreman challenged me. I told him I was doing the best I could. He flew into a furious passion, dragged me into the turning shop, cut a strap off a lathe and lashed me cruelly. He then seized me by the ears and hung me for a few moments over a window three storeys from the ground . . . Employers, excepting a few high-minded and generous men, wallowed in nought but a sea of selfishness and icy indifference. The common sympathies of humanity were crushed

by the raging passion for gold, and the pride of wealth alienated their hearts and understandings so much from the sufferings of the young and moral necessities of the poor who toiled for them, that they surely in the whirlwind of competition and avarice dreamed they were superior mortals born to trample and tyrannise over those whom necessity had placed at their command." Conditions obviously improved greatly over the next century and more under various Acts of Parliament, and although life was always hard in the mills those who worked in them enjoyed a remarkable camaraderie. And in fairness it must be pointed out that several of the jute barons endowed Dundee with many fine public facilities.

Single end.

South Union Street.

South Union Street (left) was obliterated in the mid 1960's to make way for the Tay Road Bridge and its attendant network of roads. There is little trace to be seen of what was once the hub of rail and ferry activity, a part of bustling, down-town Dundee remembered with great affection. South Union Street, a continuation of existing Union Street, stretched out along the front of the West and Tay Bridge Stations, ending at the Tay Ferries terminal where Riverside Drive sweeps westwards along the waterfront and out of the city. The constant flow of traffic to and from thc "Fifics" at Craig Picr, the steady stream of L.N.E.R. and L.M.S. passengers, and the shifting of rail freight by horse-drawn carts all contributed to a kaleidoscope of never-ending interest. One of the outstanding shops in this area was the newsagent's business run by the kenspeckle Stuart Patrick where customers were offered a range of publications unavailable elsewhere in the city at that time. Almost next door was the Waverley Temperance Hotel, only a stone's throw away from another – and more famous – "dry" establishment, Mather's Hotel, which stood opposite the West Station.

In these days hotel porters would often be at the stations to meet guests arriving by rail and take charge of their luggage. Mathers had a regular clientele of fascinating commercial travellers. One smoked cigarettes bearing his own name and another was nicknamed "Happy Days" because that was the message printed on the back of his visiting cards. There was the English "rep" who had such a high regard of the local water that he bottled several pints to take home after each visit. Another colourful character was the jewellery traveller who refused to let anyone carry his cases or help him with his coat. Curving down from the Nethergate to the foot of Union Street was Yeaman Shore (right), a fragment of which still remains today alongside the inner ring road. This old street was named after the Yeaman family of Lochee who were prominent in local civic circles, George Yeaman having served two terms as Provost in the early 1700's. Yeaman Shore, which later ran along the back of the Green's Cinema, was mainly occupied by business premises including coal merchants James Hood and Taylor Brothers; Rossleigh, the garage; and Low and Duff, engineers. The office of the Anglo-American Oil Company brought an exotic touch to an otherwise drab thoroughfare. Anyone returning to Dundee today after a long absence and looking south from the bottom of Union Street might think they were on a different planet.

Yeaman Shore.

A sight for sore eyes. Gazing across Earl Grey Dock to Dock Street and the bus terminus at Shore Terrace with the rear of the Caird Hall forming a back-drop to this well-remembered panorama. The Earl Grey was the dock used by the sandboats which landed up to 200,000 tons of sand every year from deposits in the river. In this scene several sprat boats are also in view although the city's fleet of spratters operated mainly from King William Dock further along Dock Street.

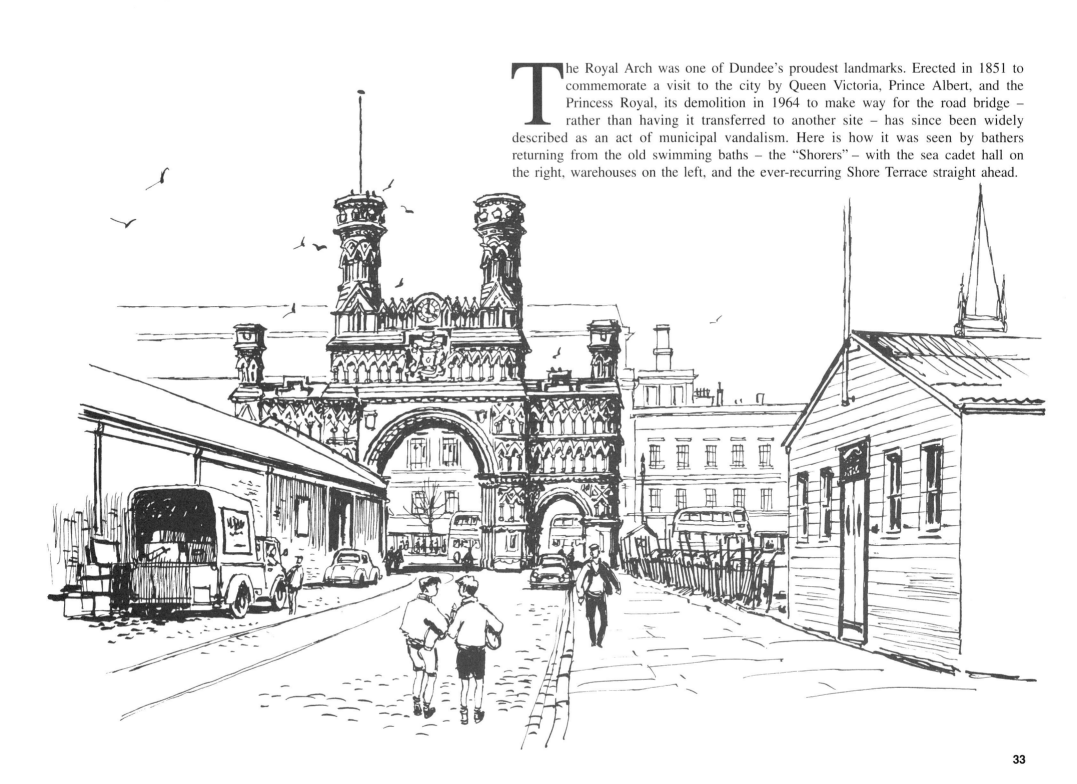

The Royal Arch was one of Dundee's proudest landmarks. Erected in 1851 to commemorate a visit to the city by Queen Victoria, Prince Albert, and the Princess Royal, its demolition in 1964 to make way for the road bridge – rather than having it transferred to another site – has since been widely described as an act of municipal vandalism. Here is how it was seen by bathers returning from the old swimming baths – the "Shorers" – with the sea cadet hall on the right, warehouses on the left, and the ever-recurring Shore Terrace straight ahead.

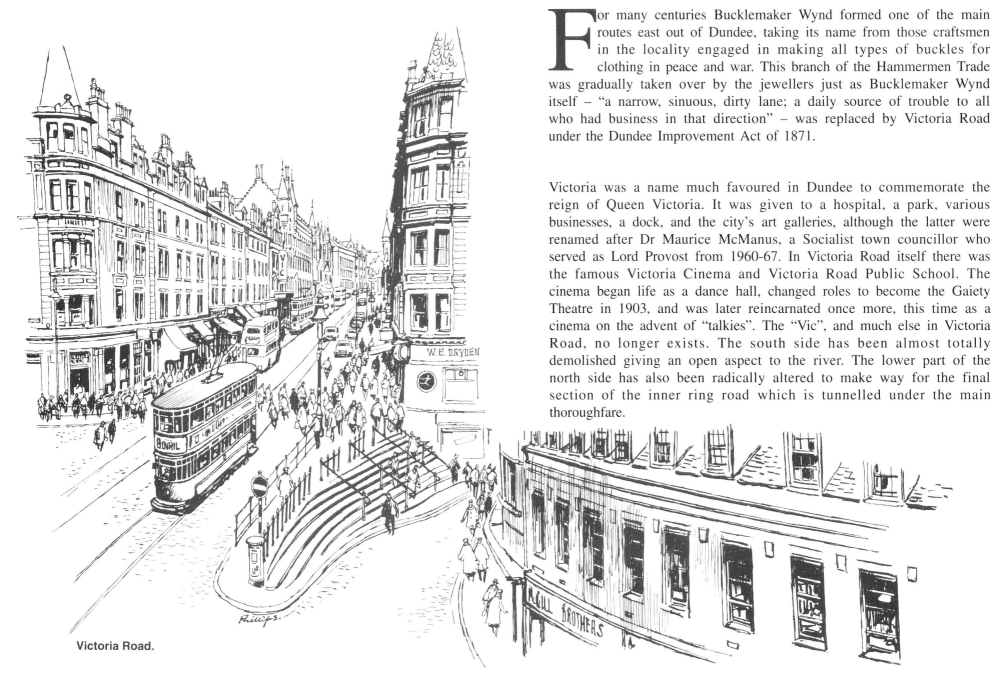

Victoria Road.

For many centuries Bucklemaker Wynd formed one of the main routes east out of Dundee, taking its name from those craftsmen in the locality engaged in making all types of buckles for clothing in peace and war. This branch of the Hammermen Trade was gradually taken over by the jewellers just as Bucklemaker Wynd itself – "a narrow, sinuous, dirty lane; a daily source of trouble to all who had business in that direction" – was replaced by Victoria Road under the Dundee Improvement Act of 1871.

Victoria was a name much favoured in Dundee to commemorate the reign of Queen Victoria. It was given to a hospital, a park, various businesses, a dock, and the city's art galleries, although the latter were renamed after Dr Maurice McManus, a Socialist town councillor who served as Lord Provost from 1960-67. In Victoria Road itself there was the famous Victoria Cinema and Victoria Road Public School. The cinema began life as a dance hall, changed roles to become the Gaiety Theatre in 1903, and was later reincarnated once more, this time as a cinema on the advent of "talkies". The "Vic", and much else in Victoria Road, no longer exists. The south side has been almost totally demolished giving an open aspect to the river. The lower part of the north side has also been radically altered to make way for the final section of the inner ring road which is tunnelled under the main thoroughfare.

In its hey-day Victoria Road was one of the city's busiest shopping centres which existed alongside a variety of industrial premises such as the jute complex of A. & S. Henry and the Forebank Dye Works. The well-known shops included Ben Forbes, the piano specialists, and Jackson, the cycle agent. B. L. Fenton, the auctioneers, are still in business today. Like other distinctive areas of the city, Victoria Road had a vibrant community spirit. Even the youngsters at the local school felt themselves somewhat superior to their counterparts at nearby Cowgate School at whom they often chanted the following verse:

The Coogate Skale's an affy skale,
It's made wi' sticks and plester,
But the only thing that bathers me
Is the bawldy-heided mester.

One of Dundee's most prominent citizens in the earlier part of this century lived up a close in the Victoria Road area. He was Edwin Scrymgeour, known to all as Neddy, who sensationally defeated Winston Churchill, then one of the city's M.P.'s, on a prohibition ticket in the election of 1922. Neddy worked as a clerk after leaving school but gave up his job to form the Prohibition Party in 1898. He was elected to the town council in 1905 and, after various unsuccessful attempts, finally reached the House of Commons seventeen years later. He proved a diligent M.P., pursuing the welfare of his constituents with the same zeal as he railled against the demon drink. Defeated in 1931, Neddy devoted himself to evangelical work in his remaining years. He died in 1947, aged 80. But his supporters' famous cry, "Vote, vote, vote, for Neddy Scrymgeour", still evokes memories of a unique Parliamentarian.

Neddy Scrymgeour.

Pinner.

Although not exactly the playing fields of Eton, the streets of Dundee provided the recreational facilities for generations of youngsters brought up in a densely-populated, industrial environment. Apart from football, cricket, and rounders, there was a whole range of other games – almost of Olympic proportions – which made use of streets and pavements, tenement buildings, and other exterior furnishings. These street games often had different names and were played under varying sets of rules, not only in different parts of Scotland but as from one district to another within Dundee. Those we mention here are merely a selection taken from a much larger repertoire. Let us start with "Pinner", one of the great favourites which was centred on a manhole or hydrant cover, often referred to as a "cundie".

A pinner was a piece of metal about 1½ inches square and could be a square washer or, ideally, a bit of an old file. This gave it the serrated surface required to prevent it from sliding or skiting off the cundie. Players would line up a short distance from the cundie and "pitch for killer". The one whose pinner landed nearest the centre of the metal cover became the first killer. Waiting until the others had pitched their pinners away from the cundie, he then attempted to hit them one at a time with his own marker. Each time he succeeded he won a "photie" (cigarette photograph). But if he failed to strike a particular pinner that player would toss for the cundie and, if successful, would then take over the role of killer. And so the game progressed, often moving from one manhole cover to another on the way to and from school.

While the boys played pinner the girls were often testing their skills at "Boxies", otherwise known as hopscotch or peevers. Here, a set of six or eight boxes were chalked out on the road or pavement. A player would then push a flat stone along the ground towards the boxes. If it finished inside a box without encroaching on a line the player would proceed to hop through the boxes to pick it up, still on one leg, then hop all the way back to base. If the player stepped on a line or put both feet on the ground they lost the round. The other variation was to push the marker with your foot from one box to another, hopping all the way and again having to avoid the lines of the boxes. "Hide and Seek" was, of course, a game where everyone joined in and here again it took different forms. As

"Kick the Can" it also made use of a manhole cover on which was placed an old tin can to act as the "block". When the can was kicked away the player who was "down" had to retrieve it while the others concealed themselves in the immediate vicinity. If the down player spied one of the others and could get back to the can first the person flushed out then had to take over the can. With "Bully Horn" a shop entrance or close-mouth was selected as the base with the down person shouting "bully horn" when they were ready to seek out the hidden players. Otherwise the same rules applied.

Boxies.

"Huckey-Duck" consisted of two teams of boys. Those in the team going "down" all crouched in leapfrog position in a line, one behind the other, the leader planting his head in the midriff of a player standing against a wall and acting as a pillow. The other team would then leap, one at a time, along the backs of the others, the first jumper having to vault on to the back of the player at the top of the line. If they all landed safely and stayed on they would shout: "Huckey-Duck, Huckey-Duck, Huckey-Duck, three times on and off again." But if anyone fell off, the down team then became the jumpers. In picking sides, for whatever team event, each captain would often recite the lines:

Eenerty, Feenerty, Ficherty Feg;
Ell, Dell, Dome-in, Egg;
Irky, Birky, Starry rock;
Ann, Tan, two's Jock.

Huckey-Duck.

Whoever the captain pointed to on the word "Jock" was duly selected for that team.

The simplest game of all was "Tig" where one player had to run after all the others until they touched someone and shouted "tig", whereupon that boy or girl became the chaser. With "High Tig" a player jumping on to anything above ground level, even climbing up a lamp-post, couldn't be touched. When it came to individual skills there were few activities more testing than "walking" the gird.

A gird was simply a metal hoop the size of a bicycle wheel, often obtained from a blacksmith. It came with a cleek, a steel rod with a hook at the end which engaged low down on the gird. By stroking and controlling the gird with the cleek the operator could run alongside at varying speeds, steering the hoop through crowded pavements without mishap. Some youngsters would run their gird for miles, taking it on an outing from outlying areas into the centre of Dundee. Marbles required a different knack. In this game each player would place an earthenware or coloured glass marble inside a circle then, drawing lots, would take it in turn to use their "plunker" to knock out the marbles one at a time, the aim being to "skin the ringey". Here, also, there were several permutations of the game. One of the favourite pastimes for girls was to run round in a circle clasping hands and singing:

Three times round goes our gallant ship,
And three times round goes she;
And three times round goes our gallant ship,
Until it sinks to the bottom of the sea. (*All squat*)

Pull her up, pull her up, cried the brave sailor boy;
Pull her up, pull her up, cried he. (*All rise*)
Pull her up, pull her up, cried the brave sailor boy,
Until he sank to the bottom of the sea. (*All down*)

"Walking" the gird.

The girls would also stot a small ball in time to a well-known piece of verse, lifting a leg over the bouncing ball at the end of each line:

> One, two, three-a-leerie,
> Four, five, six-a-leerie,
> Seven, eight, nine-a-leerie,
> Ten-a-leerie postman.

Another version went like this:

Marbles.

> One, two, three-a-leerie,
> I saw Missus Peerie,
> Sittin' on her bumbaleerie,
> Eatin' chocolate soldiers.

Street games are now virtually a thing of the past. More sophisticated pastimes, such as video games, have largely taken over. But these traditional street games would no longer be possible anyway in roadways now congested with cars and other vehicles.

"One, two, three-a-leerie . . . "

Onion Johnny.

Onion ("Ingin") Johnnies from France and fishwives from Arbroath – both sold their wares round the doors in Dundee for well over a hundred years and, in the process, became part of the social fabric of the city. The onion salesmen were from Britanny and first arrived in this country in 1828, landing a consignment of their unique Roscoff Reds at Plymouth. Led by an enterprising sailor-peasant, Henri Olivier, the Bretons soon found that their local product was more prized in London than in Paris, where the housewives preferred the yellow-skinned variety of onions. The seasonal trade gradually developed until, between the two world wars, 15,000 Onion Johnnies were cycling the length and breadth of Britain on their familiar bikes, strings of onions suspended from the handlebars. Many of the Bretons were called Jean-Yves, which soon turned into the nickname "Johnny", and from that the term "Onion Johnnies" was to take its place in the folklore of Britain. In Scotland they polished up their English with Scottish accents, very often talking in the local dialect. Some of those who covered the Dundee area operated from stables in Dock Street.

"Bonjour, Madam", was their polite greeting on the doorstep and it wasn't long before the friendly Frenchmen with their ruddy complexions and blue berets became part and parcel of the local scene from the time they arrived each August. To begin with they sailed direct to Dundee but latterly they arrived overland from other U.K. ports. Some of the Onion Johnnies brought their families across with them and many friendships were formed with local people. Sometimes they attended various social functions, such as Burns Suppers, and several of the onion men supported Dundee football teams. The onions were sold as far north as John O' Groats, drawing on a warehouse in Aberdeen where 400 tons of onions were stockpiled every autumn. When an "Ingin" Johnny failed to appear in his district at the start of the season there were always anxious enquiries about his welfare. In 1905, 74 of the Bretons were drowned in the English Channel when the steamship, Hilda, taking them home from Southampton, struck rocks near St. Malo and sank. By 1988 the Onion Johnnies had almost disappeared from the British scene, the advent of the supermarket having steadily altered the buying habits of the housewife, although it was said that the young Bretons were no longer attracted to the itinerant lifestyle of their forefathers.

The Arbroath fishwives were another great favourite on the Dundee doorstep and here again, like the onion sellers, formed lasting friendships with many of their customers. Most of the fishermen's wives had fish rounds. The fish they bought at the late afternoon auctions was delivered to work sheds at the rear of their homes and there they toiled until the small hours of the following morning, filleting and processing. They then loaded the fish into creels, two to be carried on the back and one on each arm, before setting off on their rounds after an early breakfast. The women wore dark blue skirts of heavy serge, called blue coats, which had pleats running round the calf-length garments. Dark silk blouses were gathered at the waist and covered by a shawl. They also wore a black or dark blue apron with white or grey stripes. The fishwives went into many of the Angus towns. When they travelled to Dundee by train their creels of haddock, whiting, and smokies, were "quarantined" in the guard's van. These women, some of them quite elderly, would walk for miles with their heavy loads in the course of a day's selling.

But they were always cheerful and dependable and would often be invited in for a cup of tea and something to eat. However, with the growing use of vans for delivery after the last war, the fishwives, as with the Onion Johnnies later, gradually became an institution of the past. Many other travelling sales people also came regularly to the door. There were brush salesmen, women collecting rags and old clothes, the "Spirella wifie" measuring clients for corsets, and the "Galashiels man" selling lengths of cloth for suits and dresses. For many working-class households in Dundee there was also another type of caller – the "chapper laddie" or the "chapper up". They would hammer on the doors of their customers with a heavy stick between four and six in the morning, wakening the occupants in time for work. In 1872 they were paid the princely sum of 2d a week for an early call and a penny a week for a knock nearer six o'clock. In June that year, however, the Lochee chappers threatened industrial action. Unless they were paid more they said they would allow their customers to sleep in:

> "You all know Jim, my little cousin,
> For one shilling he must rap a dozen."

Arbroath Fishwife.

Camperdown House.

Camperdown is another of the names which is much in evidence throughout Dundee. It commemorates an epic naval battle won by the son of a local family who became one of the great British admirals of the eighteenth century when Brittania indeed ruled the waves. Admiral Duncan, commanding the North Sea Fleet, defeated the Dutch in a classic and bloody engagement fought on October 11, 1797, just off the coast of Holland within sight of the small town of Camperdown. It thus became known as the Battle of Camperdown and since then the name has had an honoured place in the annals of Dundee. It has been given to streets, roads, factories, a dock, the headquarters of the R.N.V.R., a church, and a housing area. But, most impressively of all, it is the name of Dundee's finest park on the northern outskirts of the city: Camperdown Park, complete with 18-hole golf course, wildlife centre, and the outstanding classical, colonnaded mansion of Camperdown House. The house was completed in the 1820's for Robert Duncan, the admiral's son, and was purchased by the city, together with the picturesque grounds, in 1946.

Adam Duncan was born in Dundee in July, 1731. His father was Provost from 1744 until 1746, the year Adam joined the Royal Navy to serve on a sloop-of-war under the command of his cousin, and soon to see action against the French. By 1759 he had the rank of Commander with his own ship, Royal Exchange, deployed on convoy duty. At that time Duncan was reputed to be the biggest and finest man in the navy. A magazine article was later to describe him in these terms: *"He was of size and strength almost gigantic . . . 6 feet 4 inches and of corresponding breadth. As a young officer walking through the streets of Chatham his grand figure and handsome face attracted crowds of admirers."*

He was a Captain by the age of thirty and in 1787, at 56, was given the rank of Rear Admiral at a time when Britain was variously at war with France, Spain, and Holland. Having played a leading part in putting down a famous mutiny in 1797, Admiral Duncan went on later that year to immortalise himself at the Battle of Camperdown, fought in nine fathoms

of water and watched by thousands lining the Dutch coast. Had Duncan lost the French would possibly have attempted to invade Britain. But his daring tactics against a superior force won the day, a strategy profitably employed by Nelson the following year at the Battle of the Nile. Duncan's victory led to great rejoicing throughout the land. He was created a Viscount, "Admiral Lord Duncan of Camperdown", and given the Freedom of London. Later he marched in full uniform through Dundee to receive further honours from the magistrates of the city.

He retired from the navy in 1800, spending his final years quietly at Lundie House, the family home near Dundee. He died in 1804 and was buried in Lundie Churchyard. Adam Duncan, a Dundee boy, had taken his place in naval history alongside Hawke, Keppel, Howe, Rodney, Hood, Collingwood, and Nelson. As Lord Nelson wrote on Duncan's death: "The name of Duncan will never be forgotten by Britain and in particular by its navy."

Admiral Duncan.

John Mills.

Dundee is the only place in Britain to have a full-time, publicly-owned observatory offering facilities to anyone interested in astronomy – even at the most basic level – under the supervision of a professional city astronomer. The Mills Observatory, standing on the summit of Balgay Hill within Balgay Park, is therefore unique in the history of amateur astronomy in this country. It is visited every year by over 15,000 people, ranging from those only casually curious about the universe to others who are studying the subject at a more serious level. All of this has been provided through the generosity and vision of John Mills, a Dundee textile manufacturer during the last century who was also a keen amateur astronomer. He had been inspired by a fellow Dundonian, the celebrated Thomas Dick, a minister who wrote widely on astronomy in the belief that the greatness of God could best be appreciated by the study of the universe. Mills built his

own observatory on the slopes of the Law, near what is now Adelaide Place. It was equipped with a main telescope under the dome, along with other instruments which allowed him to time the passage of stars across the meridian. Nothing now remains of that building. But when he died in 1889, at the age of 83, he directed that his estate be devoted to *"the provision of a building equipped with astronomical and other instruments suitable for the study of the wonder and beauty of the works of God in Creation."* When Dundee Town Council received the bequest they went into a bit of a flat spin. There was no precedent for a public observatory being funded by private money. So the city fathers offered the cash to University College, Dundee – then part of St. Andrews University – in the hope they could fulfil the terms of John Mills's estate.

They in turn sought the advice of others, including experts at the Royal Greenwich Observatory, as to the feasibility of a "people's observatory". But there was a consensus that only very limited public access could be afforded to such a facility. This, of course, would have failed to meet the terms of the legacy and consequently the University College turned down the project. A trust was then set up in conjunction with the Town Council and plans were prepared to build the observatory on the top of Dundee Law. However, when war broke out in 1914 the undertaking was suspended and when hostilities ended the observatory site was used instead for a war memorial. It wasn't until the Depression of the 1930's that the matter was raised again, this time activated by the need to provide work for the ailing building industry.

Professor Sampson, the Astronomer Royal for Scotland, examined various sites before finally deciding that the top of Balgay Hill was by far the most favourable, both for public access and astronomical suitability, the elevated, tree-lined location protecting the observatory's seeing conditions from the glare of city lights and other forms of pollution. The building duly went ahead and was formally opened by the professor on October 28, 1935. Today, apart from its range of telescopes, the Mills Observatory is also equipped with a planetarium and an audio-visual theatre, and continues to fulfil the dream of John Mills that Dundee should play an important role in the development of amateur astronomy in Britain.

Mills Observatory.

Syd Scroggie.

Syd Scroggie has roamed the hills and mountains of Scotland, scaling the heights and exploring the corries, glens, and rugged passes. He has written books of poems about the joys and heartbreaks of tackling Mother Nature in the great outdoors, deeply-sensitive verse reflecting keen observational powers and a chuckling sense of humour. Many others have accomplished all of this too. But Syd Scroggie is special. He is totally blind and has one artificial leg. As Lieutenant W. Sydney Scroggie of the Lovat Scouts he was blown up by a land-mine in Italy only two weeks before the end of the Second World War. He swore then he would return to his beloved mountains, and so it turned out to be until even today, at the age of 73, he continues to take to the hills with his climbing companions from his cottage on the outskirts of Dundee. "What draws you there," he says, "is an inner experience, something psychological, something poetic, which perhaps cannot be fully understood when the physical aspect of things get in the way when you have your sight." In his first collection of poems, "Give Me the Hills", he included the following piece called "Ante Mortem":

> I will attempt the Capel track
> Old, stiff, and retrograde
> And get some pal to shove me on
> Should resolution fade.
>
> For I must see black Meikle Pap
> Against a starry sky
> And watch the dawn from Lochnagar
> Once more before I die.

And when Syd is finally called away he wants his burial cairn to carry the following epitaph:

> Alaw these steens there lies a lad
> Pech't oot an' fairly deen,
> He gae'd his ain gait a' his life
> But whiles wi' ithers' een.

Dundee has produced many successful writers who have churned out best-selling fiction on a lucrative scale. David Phillips was never in that category, but as a writer for over thirty years he commanded a captive following for his inimitable stories of the Dundee he grew up in and lived his entire adult life. His memories and observations of the local scene – mainly of a humorous nature – filled sixteen books, hundreds of newspaper and magazine articles, and were featured many times on radio and television programmes. His output was prodigious. He wrote mainly as he spoke, in the broad Dundee dialect known as "Dundonese" of which he was the acknowledged master in print. Here he describes the strategic importance of tenement "pletties", the platforms or landings running along the outside of the houses above street level and which were connected to the central stairway:

"Good weather brought tenants out to the pletties, to gossip, to perhaps share a pot of tea; and the pletties were natural circles and galleries to be addressed by down-at-heel evangelists, wandering minstrels, and the Salvation Army. From the pletties of many tenements you looked around at other pletties of tenements in neighbouring streets. Women made much use of this feature in communicating with friends across the greenies, and could see at a glance if their bairns were playing on pals' pletties. And being the way they are, some women took advantage of the opportunities to record the to-and-fro-ings of tenants and their friends – and others . . . 'Look, there's Erchie hingin' on the railin's again! He'll think Mag's still at her mither's – little does he ken she's back this 'oor; he'll get banjoed this nicht; Goad help him tae – he hasna much life wi' her . . . ' "

Davey also wrote full-length biographies of Dundee's famous poet William McGonagall and his life-long friend, Jimmy Shand, the accordion maestro. He spent much time stravaiging the hills and mountains of Scotland and many of his fine photographs of breath-taking vistas were both published and exhibited. David Phillips, who never married, lived alone in a council house in Lochee. When he left home on January 12, 1987, for his daily visit to the public swimming baths, he pinned the usual note to his front door giving the time he expected to be back. But on that day he never returned. He collapsed and died in Lochee High Street. He was 72.

Dave Phillips.

Dundee went into mourning on "Black Tuesday" – December 8, 1959 – when the Broughty Ferry lifeboat, Mona, capsized in a ferocious storm, losing her entire crew of eight men. She had been on her way to assist the North Carr lightship which had been torn from her moorings off Fife Ness and was drifting in heavy seas. The lifeboat never reached her. She was found five hours later, at first light, swept ashore on the sandy beach at Buddon Ness, near Carnoustie. A body was floating in the surf. Another lay on the beach half-a-mile away. Coastguards recovered five other bodies from the wheelhouse. The eighth member of the crew had been swept out to sea. The death roll read:

```
Coxswain Ronald Grant (28)

Second Coxswain George Smith (53)

Engineer John Grieve (56)

John Grieve (22), son of the engineer

Alexander Gall (56)

James Ferrier (43)

David Anderson (42)

George Watson (38)
```

In the meantime the lightship had reached the safety of St. Andrews Bay, resting a mile off-shore from Kingsbarns. Events which were to stun the nation began at 3.13 in the morning when rockets were fired to summon the Mona's crew to the lifeboat shed at the bottom of Fort Street in the old fisher quarter of Broughty Ferry. The Anstruther, Dunbar, and Arbroath lifeboats were storm-bound. But the Broughty station lay in the comparatively sheltered waters of the Tay, just up-river from the estuary. By 4.48 a.m. the lifeboat had crossed the Bar of the river, which many had expected to be the most hazardous part of the rescue mission.

At 5.8 a.m. Fife Ness Coastguard reported lack of contact with the Mona. She had simply disappeared in a turmoil of gale force winds and heavy seas. It is believed she had capsized south of the entrance to the Tay and been swept helplessly towards Buddon Ness until being righted when her signal mast scraped the river bed in shallow waters. The Mona had been launched in May 1935 and in her 24 years of service at Broughty Ferry had saved 118 lives, many of them in daring missions against formidable odds.

A previous coxswain, James Coull, won the silver medal for gallantry in December, 1939, following the rescue of nine men from the trawler, Quixotic, which had been wrecked on the Bell Rock. Three years before she had gone to the aid of another lightship, the Abertay, again at the mercy of storm-lashed seas after breaking free from her moorings in the North Sea. On that occasion she rescued the lightship crew of five. On a foggy December night in 1948 she took off the largest number of people from any one casualty – 70 passengers who had been aboard the "Fifie", Sir William High, when she became stranded on the Fowler Rock, just off Dundee's Western Pier.

The Mona also saw much action during the Second World War. In January, 1940, she rescued the 21 crew members of the steamer Stancourt which ran aground in a snowstorm on the Abertay Sands after being harried by a German aircraft. In another storm fifteen months later the Ferry lifeboat went to the aid of a Belgian liner in a south-bound convoy off the Angus coast when it also struck the notorious Bell Rock. On that occasion the 37 crew and eight passengers were picked up by the Mona. The lifeboat service at Broughty Ferry dates back to 1830, although it didn't come under the auspices of the Royal National Lifeboat Institution until 1861. The first R.N.L.I. boat went on station the following year. It was the Mary Hartley, named after a lady in Devon who raised the entire cost of £350. The bill for the lifeboat shed came to £200. The loss of the Mona brought a compassionate response from every part of the country and a disaster fund for the crew's families raised over £90,000. The proud tradition of lifeboat service at Broughty Ferry is today carried on by a vessel aptly named, "Spirit of Tayside."

"Mona" to the rescue.

Blackscroft was one of the smaller, more compact, communities in old Dundee, perched on the rise leading east out of the city with Dock Street down below and Princes Street high above. Named after Patrick Black, a 16th century burgess, this former crofting land (Black's Croft) had all the infrastructure of the other city precincts: tenements, backlands, closes, shops of every description, and a loyal body of local residents. At one time, earlier this century, the retail section included a wide range of characters. There was Fizzie Gow with her sweetie shop, Tammy Nohair and his dairy, Whusker Ned ran the general store, Willie McNab had the newsagents, Sam Cameron was the grocer, the pub was run by Kenny and the pawnshop by Mrs Strachan. Those who wanted a ha'pennyworth of syrup or treacle would take their tin round to George White, another grocer, who would duly fill it from the tap of one of his many barrels. And there was a chip shop where you could get a pennyworth of broken fish. Two of the best-known institutions in Blackscroft were the mission church and the public library,

standing side by side like sentinels as you entered the area from the Seagate end. Both were named after St. Roque who had "obtained the odour of sanctity" through his devoted ministrations to those struck down by the plague which had cursed Dundee many centuries before. The church has now been converted to offices and the library has served as a lounge bar. How times change! Like all dormitories, Blackscroft was a playground for youngsters and the local gang would regularly descend the long flight of stairs leading to Foundry Lane and there do battle with the "Foondery Laners". On their way down they would pass "The Diggings", squalid hovels reached by dark staircases and even murkier lobbies. But Blackscroft did boast of some bonny, country-like cottages with attractive window boxes lying back from the main road.

When not engaged in conflict the local lads would take their pilers down Peep o'Day Lane to the gasworks in Dock Street to collect cinders for the family fire. When they reached the "Gassie" gates and handed over fourpence their sacks were filled to the brim from a huge chute. Very often the barrows would break down under the weight of their load as the "crew" laboured back up the steep lane. But every piler had a full set of "tools" . . . nails, washers, rope, string, screws, wingnuts, and hammer. Having reached their closie the youngsters then had to heave the sacks into the house, sometimes after tottering up four flights of stairs. But in these days it was all part of life.

Coke from the "Gassie."

Blackscroft

51

Candle Lane

From early times Dundee had a network of quaintly-named lanes and wynds in the rather bleak Dock Street-Seagate area of the city where quite a number of these narrow thoroughfares can still be found today. They include Candle Lane, Mary Ann Lane, East and West Whale Lanes, Foundry Lane, Sugarhouse Wynd, Horse Wynd, and Peep o'Day Lane. Very few people lived at these addresses. They were mainly the location of warehouses, engineering workshops, and other industrial premises and their names often reflected the type of business conducted within their perimeters. Candle Lane, for example, was where candles were once made by Joseph Sanderson, who also dealt in tobacco. He established his workshop in 1780 which flourished until 1844 when candle power was replaced by gas. East and West Whale Lanes were similarly associated with whaling and it was in these twin corridors running down towards the harbour that the industry's main offices were located. Peep o'day Lane, however, does not owe its name to a particular trade.

It still runs between Blackscroft and Dock Street and was often linked to the Irish rebels of 1798 who called themselves the "Peep o'Day Boys". But this lane has a much more aristocratic pedigree. A Dundee map of 1803 clearly shows a residence at this spot called Peep o'Day Mansion. This was probably built between 1760 and 1780 by the Hon. Walter Ogilvy, of Clova, who became the sixth titular Earl of Airlie. His older brother, Lord Ogilvy, raised a Forfarshire Regiment (Forfarshire being the old name for the county of Angus) to fight for the cause of Bonnie Prince Charlie at Culloden. The mansion was later abandoned and then finally demolished when the Dundee gas works were established in Dock Street. But why Peep o'Day? Possibly because the mansion, facing east, caught the first light each morning. It was whaling, however, which once dominated this area within sight and sound of a harbour tightly packed with ships. Whaling on a proper commercial scale in Dundee began in 1754 with the launching of the Dundee Whale Fishing Company. By 1872 the city had become Britain's leading whaling port with a fleet which finally consisted of sixteen vessels crewed by 700 seamen. The vessels were built in Dundee yards and included such famous names as the Advice, Balaena, Polar Star, Narwhal, Camperdown, and the Terra Nova. The latter, bought by the government after its whaling days were over, took Captain Scott and his team of explorers on their last, fateful expedition to the South Pole in 1910-12. The city's whaling industry reached a peak in 1885 after which no more whalers were built locally and the trade went into gradual decline until the last sailings were recorded at the outbreak of the First World War. By then whale oil had been replaced by mineral oil in a large range of manufacturing processes – including the softening of raw jute – and profit now largely depended on the yield of whale bone. But the Dundee fleet had failed to re-equip itself with modern technology to meet the changing nature of the industry. Long before its demise, however, there had been great excitement in home waters in December, 1883, when a huge, humpback whale, following shoals of sprats and herring, finished up in the Tay. Crowds turned out along the river bank to view this monster of the deep which the local fleet normally had to sail hundreds of miles to find inside the Arctic Circle. Several vessels left the harbour to display their catching skills in front of a home crowd. They scored several direct hits with their harpoons but the whale dragged the ships across the estuary before breaking free of the lines and escaping out to sea. The whaling crews returned to port amid much embarrassment. Several days later, however, the dead whale was found floating off Inverbervie by a Gourdon fishing boat and towed into Stonehaven. The carcass was auctioned off for £226 to a Dundee oil merchant, John Woods, who had it brought back to the city and put on display by public demand. Fifty thousand people – many brought to the city by rail and bus excursions – paid an admission charge of a shilling or sixpence, depending on the time of day, to view the catch and earn its owner a huge profit on his transaction. Professional photographers snapped visitors sitting in the jacked-open jaws of the famous Tay whale. McGonagall recorded the episode thus:

'Twas in the month of December, and in the year 1883
That a monster whale came to Dundee,
Resolved for a few days to sport and play,
And devour the small fishes in the silvery Tay . . .

Hunting the Tay Whale.

Gellatly Street.

Gellatly Street has never been one of Dundee's most handsome thoroughfares. Indeed, it was always a pretty drab place – and still is. But despite this it was known to almost every Dundonian and for thousands it was, sadly, a place of regular pilgrimage. For here, at the bottom of this corridor running from the Seagate down to Dock Street, stood one of the city's most important buildings – the Labour Exchange, the "Broo" by any other name, where the jobless queued up twice a week to sign the unemployment register and draw their dole money. Today there are Job Centres and Social Security offices. In the old days it was simply the "Broo", the local expression for bureau as in the original Labour Bureau. Money to pay the dole was drawn each week from a city bank. On one memorable occasion the bank official responsible for the safe had left the key at home in Newport. These were the days before the road bridge and so, with hordes of impatient men crowded inside the Exchange building, the official was forced to catch a "Fifie" across the river to fetch the key from his house. By the time the money was delivered the dole queue was almost along at the Royal Arch. By 1880 Gellatly Street had degenerated into a dilapidated passageway, its junction with Seagate so narrow as to make it impassable to carts and carriages while muddy conditions underfoot made it unpopular to pedestrians. In that year, therefore, the top end of the street was demolished and widened and then rebuilt with a new complex of high buildings to match the imposing architecture of nearby Commercial Street. But latterly it became a humdrum stretch of tenements and today much of it has disappeared with the west side almost entirely an open-air car park. But in the days of whaling Gellatly Street was a bustling place, an important commercial sector of the city. Many of the tenements housed the whalers' captains, their mates, bo'sons, and carpenters, and when the fleet returned to port with a good catch there was much revelry in the area. The east side of the street was mainly occupied by the whaling trades: blacksmiths, coopers, sailmakers, ship chandlers, along with various sheds for the storage of ships' gear and provisions. At the bottom, on the corner with Dock Street where later came the Labour Exchange, there was the "Quarter-Deck Walk". Here the old salts would promenade to and fro', recounting their days at sea. But it was the "Broo" that latterly put Gellatly Street on the map:

"We're the lads fae the Tap o' the Hill,
We've never worked an wi never will."

Three of Dundee's best-known streets, each with a royal connotation, run in a continuous line all the way from Stobswell to the Cowgate. They are Albert Street, Princes Street, and King Street. All have changed considerably in recent years. Much of Princes Street has been knocked down to give an impressive vista of the river as you curve downhill towards Baxter's Mill, now converted into a complex of flats set in an attractive courtyard development which has won national awards for design and lay-out. King Street, seen here below, is now intersected near the bottom by the recently-completed inner ring road, very nearly at the point where once stood the street's famous shopping arcade. A century ago this flourishing retail centre was advertised in a regular series of handbills called "The King Street Rocket". They told of John Prophet's umbrellas giving "good cover" and featured the latest novelties in handles. Paul, the book seller and general stationer, offered pew and pocket bibles while music seller John Murdoch boasted international status as European sole agent for the Angelus organ, as well as being the only place in Britain which stocked the famous Hadyn saloon pianos. These could be bought by the firm's own hire purchase system which, according to the advert, "will be found very convenient in these dull times." And which gentleman going thin on top could repay their debt to James Anderson, the pharmacist, whose vegetable extract claimed to cure baldness at a shilling (5p) a bottle. Later one of King Street's leading establishments was the car hire firm of W. P. Robertson whose grand limousines whisked many a bride off to church on her day of days. A Robertson car added much lustre to the matrimonial scene. Indeed, it was Robertson's who introduced the concept of car hire for special occasions to Dundee in 1910, eventually building up a fleet of thirty cars. Further up King Street there was one of Dundee's most famous churches, Wishart Memorial Church, named after the great martyred reformer, George Wishart, whose preaching and work among the poor and sick had made such a mark on the city in the 16th century. Wishart Church was where mill worker Mary Slessor had worshipped before leaving for Africa to become a famous missionary in Calabar. The original Wishart Church was built in the Cowgate in 1841 then relocated sixty years later in King Street in 1901. It ceased being a church in 1975, the building now being used as a multi-purpose social centre.

King Street.

Greenmarket.

The Greenmarket was one of the great hubs of Dundee, an open-air shopping centre at the foot of the town which at certain times of the year was transformed into a huge carnival area. Here on a Saturday working-class families would throng the stalls, booths, and side shows, to create a colourful and noisy precinct. Later the "Market" was renamed Shore Terrace, running along the rear of the Caird Hall and becoming just as well-known to latter generations as the location of the Corporation bus terminus. On certain days of the week the Greenmarket was laid out with bric-a-brac and clothes stalls with the food and fruit stands moving in for the big weekend crowds. But it was during the summer holidays and at New Year – and when the Lady Mary Fair came each August – that the Greenmarket became one vast carnival, the piazza crammed with a festive multitude which spilled across Dock Street and through the Royal Arch.

The air was filled with steam organ music, the frantic voices of auctioneers, the crack of rifles in the shooting galleries, and the constant grinding and hissing of machinery as the hobby horses and the "big switchies" – the golden gondolas on the circular up and down track – conveyed their passengers into a wonderland of fun and fantasy. And the smells! The scents of oranges and grapes mixed with the aromas of kippers, smokies, and partans, all topped off with the enticing odours of the buster stalls, their owners in greasy aprons hollering, "Roll up – big peas an' lang tatties." You could refresh yourself with glasses of Boston Cream and Sarsparilla, enjoy a bag of whelks or a poke of horehound.

There were booths advertising "The Fat lady", "The Human Skeleton", and "The Dancing Bushman", and you could buy almost any commodity from a range of hucksters, cheapjacks, and quacks. In 1870 a newspaper described the Greenmarket scene on a Saturday night in these words: *"There you will see the grim struggle of the seller and the purchaser to keep the wolf from the door . . . a gathering of things animate and inanimate. Such a blending of the useful and the useless, the eatable and the uneatable, the wholesome and unwholesome, can only be found where struggling industry and poverty meet to cater for the necessities of life."* But today this part of Dundee has changed beyond all recognition as our contemporary drawing of the area shows only too clearly. The Greenmarket has long since gone (although its name has been given to a new development area just behind the railway station) and Shore Terrace

(below), now without its bus station and milling passengers, is more or less a backwater dominated by the towering concrete headquarters of Tayside Regional Council, a human filing cabinet for the local authority staff who help in the running of municipal affairs.

Shore Terrace today.

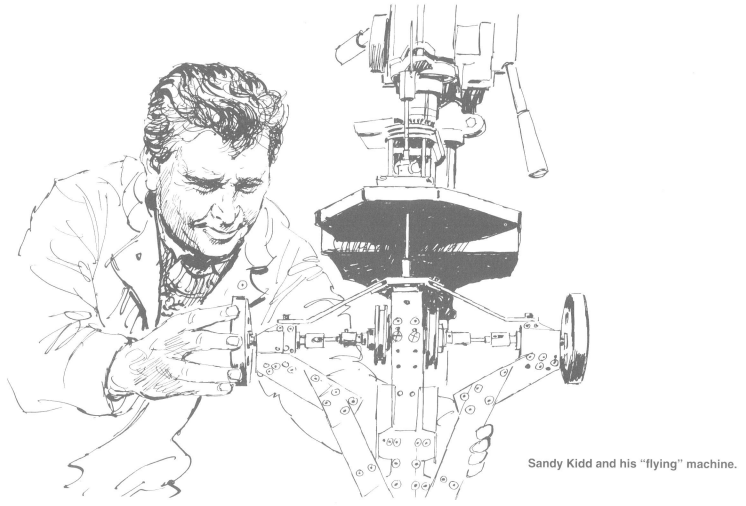

Sandy Kidd and his "flying" machine.

No story has emerged from Dundee in recent times which has so excited the imagination of people world-wide than the tale of Sandy Kidd and his "flying saucer" machine. After several years of solitary confinement in his garden shed workshop this local engineer emerged at the end of 1984 with a gyroscopic propulsion unit which he claimed would one day change the world by allowing man to cross his last frontier and explore the outer reaches of the universe. His invention caused a sensation. After a spell of research at Dundee University, Sandy and his machine were whisked off to Australia where the prototype was further developed and tested over the next two years with the backing of an international company based in Melbourne. Later his unique device was examined by boffins at British Aerospace. The Kidd Machine, as it is now known in international scientific circles, contradicts the accepted physics of Isaac Newton by claiming the principle of generating lightning speed in defiance of gravity without the need to react on air, water, or solid surface. For example, the 60 million miles to Mars would be covered in only 34 hours. We are talking here about flying saucers, and it was the possibility of such an earth-shattering development that led Sandy Kidd and his invention to be featured all over the world on television and radio, in newspapers and magazines. The garden shed engineer who was reaching for the stars also became the subject of a song and a pop video. His story has been told in a television documentary, "The Man Who Wants to Change the World", and in a book, "Beyond 2001". Today he is still working on his revolutionary project, determined that some day it will yet fulfil all its earlier promise and add even more lustre to a city of considerable accomplishment.

ACKNOWLEDGEMENTS

The authors wish to thank all those who helped in the compilation of this book, particularly the staff of the Local History Department at Dundee City Library and D. C. Thomson & Co. Ltd.